# Bumples, fumdidlers, and Jelly Beans

## Arnold Spilka

Houghton Mifflin Company　　Boston　1996

Walter Lorraine *wl* Books

Copyright © 1996 by Arnold Spilka

All rights reserved. For information about permission to
reproduce selections from this book, write to Permissions,
Houghton Mifflin Company, 215 Park Avenue South,
New York, New York 10003.

For information about this and other Houghton Mifflin trade and
reference books and multimedia products, visit The Bookstore at
Houghton Mifflin on the World Wide Web at
http://www.hmco.com/trade.

Printed in U.S.A.

WOZ  10  9  8  7  6  5  4  3  2  1

Library of Congress Cataloging-in-Publication Data

Spilka, Arnold.
  Bumples, fumdidlers and jellybeans: a grab bag of nonsense
written and illustrated by Arnold Spilka.
      p.  cm.
  Summary: A collection of nonsense poetry featuring bumple
snigglefritzers, crazy grammar, and some philosophical conundrums.
  ISBN 0-395-74522-5
  Nonsense verses, American.   2. Children's poetry, American.
[1. Nonsense verses. 2. American poetry.]   I. Title.
PS3569.P538B86   1996
811' .54—dc20                                           95-53156
                                                          CIP
                                                          AC

*For*
MICHAEL
*of*
*blessed memory*

Are you a fumdidler?
Poppin-poops are fumdidlers
who flamber flibbery flowers,
tickle tired tigers,
monkeyshine miserable monkeys,
spray soda on snoopy sparrows,
clobber cross-eyed crocodiles,
lift eleven elephants when they're
      not looking,
piddle pop-eyed poodles
and filcher foolish flies.
Are you a fumdidler?

Ducks'll quack,
Cows'll moo,
Pigs'll squeal,
What'll *you*?

The phone rang
so I said, "Hello."
"Moo," said a voice.
"Moo who?" I asked.
"Moo moo," said the voice.
"You have the wrong number," I said.
"Moo moo, ma moo moo," said the voice.
So I ordered a quart of milk and hung up.

The phone rang again.
"Hello," I said.
"Meow," said the voice.
So I ordered three kittens,
"Quack Quack Quack," said the voice.
"Send a dozen eggs," I said.
"Make up your mind," said the voice.
"Moo," I said.
"Moo who?" asked the voice.
"Why are you crying?" I asked.
"I didn't say 'Boo hoo,'" said the voice.
"Moo moo?" I asked.
"Meow Quack Moo," said the voice.
So I ordered a strawberry shortcake
    smothered with pickles and mustard
        and hung up.

Nothing matters
and everything does.
And why should I care
if my nose has fuzz
and my teeth stick out
and my cousin is fat
and my dog is a cat
and it's raining mud
and my nose is red
and my horse won't fly
though I don't know why
when I stand on my head.
And why should I care
if I'm good or bad,
If I'm smart or not.
Should I be sad
or mad
or silly?
Does anything matter
or does everything not?
Does anyone care
whatever I am
or do,
or say,
Whatever I be.
Does anyone care?
Yes . . .
ME!

There are some things
you should do sometimes.
And some things
    you should not do sometimes at all,
and those things you
    should not always do sometimes,
You must always sometimes do,
especially those sometimes things
that are not things
that sometimes you should
and would not do because
always there are reasons
    to
        ... not do
            sometimes ...
Isn't that right?

GROBBLE
GROBBLE
GROBBLE

Bumple snigglefritzers,
Are not really bumple snigglefritzers.
They are really schwizzers who want to show off.
So they cover their heads with lobular zilchers
and fly around yelling "GROBBLE GROBBLE GROBBLE"
while they eat watermelons made of spaghetti.
But that doesn't fool anybody,
because no grobble eats watermelons
unless there is candy inside.

On the other hand,
there are filchy greeps who will eat anything
even if it's not candy,
unless it's their birthday
and their mothers are watching.
then they look like bumple snigglefritzers
    who are sick
and they can't sing at all,
except when they're in school,
studying how to be finchers made of criff-criff,
but if spaghetti gets in their noses,
they go home disgusted!
    ANY QUESTIONS?

*Can you lift eleven elephants when they're not looking?*
*How about giraffes–no? Even if I gave you a kiss?*

Melissa likes me!
Yes it's true!
Yes she do!
She gave me 3 jelly beans
then took back 2,
gave me 10 more
and took back 1.
Kissed me once
and took back 10.
I'm crazy about jelly beans!

I gotta admit
trying, isn't <u>doing</u>,
but it is <u>something</u>
and something isn't <u>everything</u>
but at least it's a <u>start</u>!
I know! I know!
A start isn't a <u>finish</u>
but it is <u>trying</u>
and trying isn't...
but we did that already.

I
never
shoulda
oughta
did
some things
I
shouldn't
hadda
done,
but if
I hadn't ever
did
the oughtn't
hadda
ever had,
I wouldn't now
know
what I done
and why
I shouldn't
never
had.

So what I shouldn't never hadda,
even though I didn't wanna,
that I did and shouldn't oughta,
I never mighta ever woulda.

*Do you think filchy greeps will eat anything?*
*How about criff-criff?...Would you?*

So I said what did you say?
And she said I didn't say.
And I said do you mean you didn't say what I say
    you said you didn't say?
And she said I didn't say what I say I didn't say.
You didn't?
I *did*! *You* didn't
No! *You* did, *I* didn't!
DID DID DIDDLY DIDDLE *DIDDN'T*!
*YUM TIDDLY TUM TUM*
    ***DID DID DID***!

Don't believe anybody who says I'm mean!
It happens that I'm lovable.
  In fact I'm lovabububle!
And I'm not fat!
  Just bububububububle,
I never argue!
  I just like to quibububububububle!
    because I'm very sensibubububububububle,
And to say I'm rotten
  is absolutely laughabububububububle!
But when I sing,
    or dance,
      or whistle,
I confess I'm terribububububububule!

I sat upon a star last night
And kissed the moon
    upon his nose.
And from a passing cloud
    I took a little bite,
it tasted like the most wonderful
    ice cream,
all creamy white!
So I woke up
    rushed to the fridge,
and ate the real thing!

*If the voice on the phone says "moo" would you order*
*three kittens or a strawberry shortcake with mustard?*

"Sit down!" said the daisy.
And the tiger sat down.

"How did you do it?"
asked the buttercup.

"I told him I was an elephant,"
said the daisy.

Mushrooms are umbrellas
for
ladybugs
and
their
fellas.

Any when
some who is friendly,
there's no why
to wonder at,
where can really be
just any,
every who
is sometimes that.

A skunk stood next to a rock
"Am I not beautiful?"
asked the skunk.
The rock didn't answer.
"SPEAK," demanded the skunk,
"am I not beautiful?"
The stone didn't answer,
did not make a sound
but quickly ran away.

"I don't like you!" said Fred.

"What's the problem?" asked Sam.

"*That* is the problem!" said Fred.

"Do you mean that that is what that is
   the problem?" asked Sam.

"Yes! That is what that is the which is the problem," said Fred.

"Which is what?" asked Sam.

"That is what which!" said Fred.

"Do you mean because what is which what which is what?" asked Sam.

"Yes! So why is the problem which what that is!" said Fred.

"When?" asked Sam.

"When that is where that which is the problem
   is what!" said Fred.

"That which?" asked Sam.

"Yes, but only sometimes!" said Fred.

"When?" asked Sam.

"When that is where that which is the problem
   where what is which!" said Fred.

"Which what?" asked Sam.

"The which what is the problem which what what
   what is!" said Fred.

"Even when it's raining?" asked Sam.

"Raining where?" asked Fred.

"Raining where what when why is the problem!" said Sam.

"Even if I have an umbrella?" asked Fred.

"I'm not sure," said Sam.

"Then don't ask such stupid questions!" said Fred.

*Yum tiddlytum tum did! did! dit! Does everything not?*

If now...
Or then...
And just because
someone is here,
or there, should someone else
then have to be?
Or know?
Or even care?

Wherever is a magical place
where all of us are
 and everything is
 and yet not quite!
Where nothing matters
 and everything does,
where nothing is so
 and everything is.

When you're feeling sort of kind of,
on a somewhat sort of day
and there aren't sometimes any
reasons why there's what to say.
And you know that no one hardly
thinks that what is why is best,
and then someone says "Well ... maybe"
and there's mud across your chest!
Do you sing a song of popcorn
and a pocket full of hay,
just because you're feeling kind of
on a somewhat sort of day?

Pretty,
pesky,
Allegra Beth.
She is two years old.
O yeth! Oh yeth!
And what can you say
to a two year old?
That she is smarter than some?
That her ears are old
    and sometimes fold?
That the sun is paper?
And the moon is cake?
That clouds are custard?
And trees are fake?
That people are birds
    who cannot fly?
And cows give popcorn
    when they really try?
And it's all quite true?
Why would I lie?

"Look before you leap,"
they say.
So I looked
and then I leaped!
OUCH!
I shouldn't have listened to them!

*When it's raining does Fred know which what that is?*
*How about sometimes always?*

CLUCK!
CLUCK!

The general looked at his watch,
clucked like a hen,
kissed his elbows,
and looked again!
"Help!" he cried.
It's half-past June.
If I don't hurry,
I'll be back too soon!
And before he could think
or knew what he meant,
he jumped on his back,
and was gone where he went!

Strange things happen
when you eat a purple pill!
Your nose keeps falling off,
your neck becomes five feet long,
your ears hang down,
    scraping the ground,
and your tongue blows up
    like a big balloon!
Have you taken your
purple pill today?

How many fips in a boggle of dots?
How many lobs in a whopper?
How many gumps in a drizzle of drips?
How many pips in a popper?
Here are some hints....
A fip is a lob eating gump of a drip.
A lob is a gump drippy pip.
A gump is a lump of dotty old lob,
and a pip is a drip gumpy fimp.
But that's all for now,
though there's much more to tell.
I've a date with a frog
in a gump drippy well.

My dog ate a box of gumpy drips,
three lopcop whoppers,
a pickle fliz,
and then he sneezed in my face.
So I had him arrested!

When the clown is sick,
he calls his wife
and she butters his head
with her buttery knife.
Then she pours some jam
and plants a rose
along with baked beans
on the tip of his nose.
Do you want to know why?
Then just ask his wife
and she'll butter your head
with her buttery knife.

Eating is something I do very well,
and I never took a lesson in my life!
  Ice-cream,
    cake,
      candy,
        cookies,
  and all that stuff.
I just put them all under my nose
  AND DOWN THEY GOES!!

Milly went walking,
chased the sun,
ate a cloud,
kissed a bird,
scratched a snake,
kicked a bear.
Then went home,
feeling blue,
told her mother
she had nothing to do.

Love is a loud noise.
Flowers laugh all the time.
Play is all the colors.

*At half past june he said cluck cluck cluck*
*and he found his nose was buttered.*

By George
there was nothing to see
and yet I saw it!
Nothing to hear,
but I heard it!
I had nothing to do
so I did it!
Nothing to say
so I naturally said it!
And nothing to read
so how come you read it?

Ahhh
    Mosquitoes,
how beautiful they are,
    dancing lightly,
daintily,
    delicately humming,
talking gently to you,
    musical secrets in your ear
        SWAT!!

Butterflies ask a lot of questions
and never wait for answers.

Bees have a lot of answers
but never wait for questions.

Will there always be bees?
   … and what about cows?
Can't we make machines that can do
   what bees do?
And what's so great about milk
   and all the rest of that stuff
   like trees and buttercups?
Can't we make prettier ones out of plastic?

To build a house
First you need a large bundle of air,
some birds, mostly small,
the smell of flowers and trees,
baskets of colors,
balloons full of laughter,
and a sky within you.
That's all you need.

I didn't ask the stars to shine
    or rain to fall,
    the sun to waken me,
    or birds to look at me,
although they do.
I didn't ask my brother
    why he knew what I forgot,
or what my father dreamed
    when he would bounce me on his knee,
or what my mother thought
    before I was.
I never ask what love is...
    I just know.

A dream is tomorrow
today.

A dream is a star
that needs seeing.

A dream is a seed
that needs being.